Contents

New words

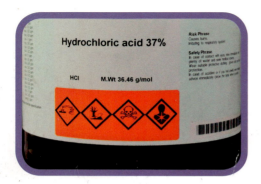

acid

claw

fight
(noun and verb)

hunt
(verb)

ill

insect

DO YOU KNOW?

Level 3

CLEVER PREY

Inspired by BBC Earth TV series and developed with input from BBC Earth natural history specialists

Written by Camilla de la Bedoyere
Text adapted by Nick Coates
Series Editor: Nick Coates

LADYBIRD BOOKS

UK | USA | Canada | Ireland | Australia
India | New Zealand | South Africa

Ladybird Books is part of the Penguin Random House group of companies
whose addresses can be found at global.penguinrandomhouse.com.
www.penguin.co.uk   www.puffin.co.uk   www.ladybird.co.uk

Penguin
Random House
UK

First published 2020
001

Printed in China

A CIP catalogue record for this book is available from the British Library

ISBN: 978-0-241-38286-8

All correspondence to:
Ladybird Books Ltd
Penguin Random House Children's
One Embassy Gardens, New Union Square
5 Nine Elms Lane, London SW8 5DA

skin

spot

spray
(verb)

strike
(verb)

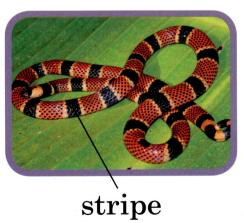

stripe

venom

How do animals stay safe?

Some animals eat other animals. They **hunt** the animals to eat them.

An animal that hunts is called a predator. The animal it catches is called the prey.

The prey tries to stay safe.

Some prey use their teeth and **claws** to stop predators.

These sea slugs use colour to tell predators, "Go away!"

WATCH!

Watch the video (see page 32).
Are the cuttlefish and crab:
a) predators?   b) prey?   c) both?

Which animal can hurt a lion?

Lions can kill a buffalo, but buffaloes are big and strong, too.

Buffaloes don't like lions.

Buffaloes sometimes try to hurt lion cubs.

The lion mother can make a lot of noise.

The lion mother can **strike** the buffalo with her claws.

The buffalo leaves, and the lion cubs are safe!

FIND OUT!

A group of lions is called a pride. **Use books or the internet** to find out what a group of buffaloes is called.

Which animals kick hard?

The giraffe is the tallest animal in the world. It can run fast, and it can kick hard.

Hungry lions can hunt and eat a giraffe. But the giraffe uses its long, strong legs to kick the lion.

Kangaroos use their strong legs to jump and kick. They can **fight** other kangaroos and stay safe from predators, too.

Dingoes hunt kangaroos.

📖 **FIND OUT!**

Use books or the internet to find out what other body parts kangaroos can use to stay safe.

Which animal can fight a jaguar?

Jaguars are big, strong cats.
Caimans are strong animals, too.

Jaguars visit the river
to look for food.

The jaguar can see
an animal in the water.

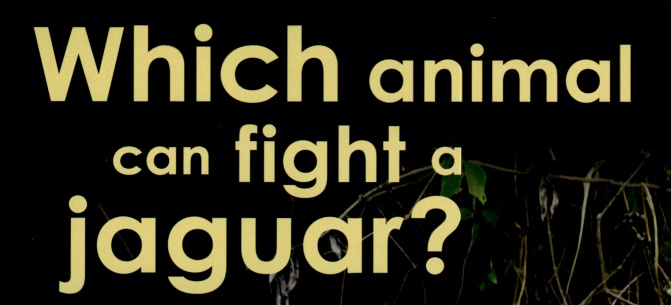

It is a caiman.

The jaguar jumps in the water.

The jaguar and the caiman are both big, strong predators. They fight.

The jaguar wins.
It kills its prey. Now, it can eat.

LOOK!

Look at the pages.
Where does the jaguar
go to get the caiman?

13

How do animals use claws and teeth?

Baboons are a kind of monkey.

Leopards and other animals hunt baboons, but the baboons use their big teeth to keep the predators away!

Animals also use their claws to stay safe.

An elephant's tusks are very long teeth. It uses its tusks to move trees and find food, but it also uses them to fight lions.

A warthog has tusks, too.

tusks

An armadillo uses its long claws to find food, but it also uses them to keep predators away.

 **THINK!**

Would you like long claws or big teeth? Why?

This is a porcupine.
It has long spines.

spines

When a predator gets close, the
porcupine's spines stand up.

Sea urchins are animals
that live in the sea.
They have spines, too.

This crab has strong claws.

A rhino is heavy and can run fast. It can hurt a lion.

horn

This rhino has a horn. A rhino's horn is hard and strong.

PROJECT

Work in a group.
Find three other animals that use their claws or teeth to defend themselves.

HOW do frogs stay safe?

Frogs don't have teeth, spines or claws. But some frogs have their **skin** to help them stay safe.

Their skin is wet, and it is horrible to eat.

Sometimes predators start to eat the frogs, but they soon stop.

The skin of poison arrow frogs can kill big animals. It can kill people, too!

A poison arrow frog is very small. It is smaller than your finger.

Poison arrow frogs live where it is hot and wet.

PROJECT

Work in a group.
Find out about poison arrow frogs. Make a poster to show some different types of poison arrow frog.

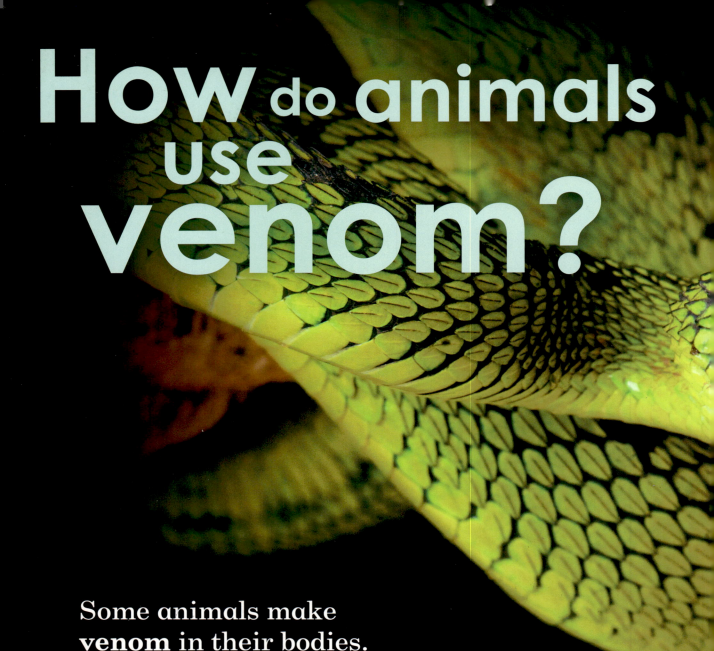

How do animals use venom?

Some animals make **venom** in their bodies.

They can use it to catch prey or to stop predators.

They can put their venom into other animals with their teeth or spines.

The venom makes the other animal feel ill. Sometimes it can kill the animal.

Some snakes use venom. They have fangs for putting the venom into their prey.

fang

A scorpion has venom in its tail.

📖 **FIND OUT!**

Snakes and lizards are both types of reptile. **Use books or the internet** to find out if any lizards use venom, too.

21

These animals use venom to stay safe.

A honeybee puts venom into a predator with its tail. The bee dies, but then the other bees are safe.

This is a wandering spider. It has very strong venom and can make a person ill.

Wandering spiders can be bigger than your hand!

Most spiders can't hurt you, but some of them carry venom. They use it to kill prey or to stop predators.

▶ WATCH!

Watch the video (see page 32).
Where does the scorpion strike the bat?
Who wins the fight?

Which animals want to be bigger?

Some animals try to look big and strong to stay safe.

Birds use their feathers and open their wings to look big.

feather

This lizard has some thin skin on its neck. The skin stands up, and the lizard opens its mouth. It looks bigger!

When a porcupinefish sees a predator, it drinks water. It gets bigger, and its spines stand up.

Now it is difficult to eat the porcupinefish!

THINK!

How is a porcupinefish the same as a porcupine, do you think?

How do insects stay safe?

This is a bombardier beetle. It uses its bottom to stay safe!

The beetle makes **acid** inside its body and **sprays** it from its bottom. The acid hurts the other animals!

Ants are small, but they can hurt animals, too.

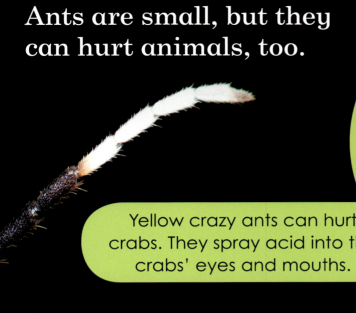

Yellow crazy ants can hurt crabs. They spray acid into the crabs' eyes and mouths.

This **insect** is a wasp.

It uses venom to keep predators away.

 WATCH!

Watch the video (see page 32).
The weaver ants must defend their home.
How do they stay safe?

What do colours say to animals?

Some colours tell animals to go away.

Red, yellow and orange
are colours that say,
"Don't eat me!"

Sea slugs use
colours to say,
"I can hurt you."

These animals use stripes or spots to tell animals not to eat them.

Bees and wasps have yellow stripes.

Ladybirds have spots. The spots tell birds, "I'm not good to eat."

FIND OUT!

Use books or the internet to find a photo of a lionfish. Draw a picture of it. Do you think it would be safe to touch a lionfish?

Quiz

Choose the correct answers.

1 Which sentence is NOT true?
  a A buffalo can hurt lion cubs.
  b A lion can kill a buffalo.
  c Buffaloes have claws.

2 A dingo is a kind of . . .
  a dog.
  b giraffe.
  c kangaroo.

3 Both giraffes and kangaroos . . .
  a can jump high.
  b have strong legs.
  c have long necks.

4 Why do jaguars visit the river?
  a to fight
  b to drink the water
  c to look for food

5 An elephant does NOT use its tusks to . . .
  a drink water.
  b fight lions.
  c find food.

6 What keeps some frogs safe?
  a their claws
  b their skin
  c their spines

7 How does a porcupinefish get bigger when it sees a predator?
  a It drinks water.
  b It eats food.
  c It stands up.

8 Spots and stripes tell a predator that the prey . . .
  a is hungry.
  b is good to eat.
  c is not good to eat.

Visit www.ladybirdeducation.co.uk for FREE DO YOU KNOW? teaching resources.

- video clips with simplified voiceover and subtitles
- video and comprehension activities
- class projects and lesson plans
- audio recording of every book
- digital version of every book
- full answer keys

To access video clips, audio tracks and digital books:

1 Go to **www.ladybirdeducation.co.uk**
2 Click "Unlock book"
3 Enter the code below

XIelSvUdRH

Stay safe online! Some of the DO YOU KNOW? activities ask children to do extra research online. Remember:

- ensure an adult is supervising;
- use established search engines such as Google or Kiddle;
- children should never share personal details, such as name, home or school address, telephone number or photos.